How to

Buy Gold and Silver;

Even when you have very little

money

by

Michael A. Tucker

Disclaimer

The opinions and information contained in this book
are based on the knowledge, understanding,
and beliefs of the author.

Every effort has been made to accurately
represent all information contained
within these pages.

Author cannot guarantee success level,
profits or final results in any way:
nor be responsible for the
actions of the reader.

Table of Contents

Tips with sound advice
- Realize gold and silver are volatile
- Avoid advice from ill informed friends
- Don't ask a financial expert if you should buy gold and silver
- Develop the habit
- Pay yourself first
- Aim to own 10-20% of your net worth in precious metals
- Once you own it, keep it

Tips on purchasing
- Start small
- Purchase old silver coins
- Use dollar cost averaging
- Buy on the dips
- Play the game 'dry' first

Tips on Dealers and Products
- Buy known brand products
- Use Reputable Dealers
- Know what you want
- Know your spot price
- Watch your premiums
- Know all purchasing costs

Storing Your Precious Metals
- Loose lips sink ships
- Safe Deposit Boxes
- Hiding at home

When to Stop Buying

Conclusion

Introduction

For whatever reason, you've decided that it would be to yours and your family's benefit to start purchasing some precious metals; commonly referred to as gold and silver. This awakening may stem from your subconscious, possibly rooted in childhood memories of Grandpa at the Sunday dinner table, talking about gold being real money, and how everybody should own some. Or maybe your decision is derived from the current financial debt and overspending that most countries are facing, forcing you to face the reality that potential financial calamity is near. Or quite possible, you noticed that the world population keeps growing and their needs keep pushing up the price of oil, food, cotton, energy, and every other natural resource known to man, and you realized precious metals have to rise in value also.

Then again, maybe I'm reading too much into your new desire for precious metals. Maybe it's nothing more than you remember that the kings in your childhood fairy tales were always surrounded by, and fighting for, gold and silver, and so you've suddenly developed a liking for the shiny stuff. Whatever the reason for your wanting to accumulate gold and silver, BRAVO! You are making one of the most sound, positive financial decisions you will make this decade, whether you realize it or not.

Once I understood the importance of adding gold and silver to my portfolio, the realization to buy hit me like a fast moving freight train. I was instantly on board. Unfortunately, at that time I also realized I faced a couple of obstacles that needed to be addressed before I could proceed. My guess is that many of you are probably facing those very same issues.

Like me, you may have very little money for making precious metal purchases; or if you *are* lucky enough to have ready cash, you're probably unsure on how to get started. Am I right?

Fear not! I was in those exact same shoes just a few short years ago. But after some research, coupled with a little knowledge, determination, and persistence, I eventually figured out that buying gold and silver was as easy as purchasing a book on Amazon or buying meat at the local grocery. I kid you not, it is really that easy! And once I discovered this information, I was able to start amassing a small fortune of the shiny collectable metals.

So in a nutshell, that's what this book is all about; empowering you with the knowledge and confidence to go out and acquire your own precious metal portfolio, because if I can pull it off, so can you.

To better assist you on this quest for knowledge, I have divided this book into two sections. *Part I* leans toward the economical reasons for purchasing precious metals. I begin by reassuring you why, in today's economical and industrial climate, gold and silver are one of the absolute strongest investments you can make. I also cover what types of gold and silver products are available to you, and explain their prices and premiums.

Part II ties in with the title of this book. Here is where I give you multiple tips on funding, purchasing, protecting, and selling your precious metals. After you are finished reading this book, I challenge you to go out and begin building your precious metal holdings to the point where you feel like those kings in your childhood fairy tales.

I took the challenge and I feel like a king!

Part I

Let me reassure you

Before I offer tips to better purchase gold and silver, let me quickly reassure you that buying precious metals at this time is a wise and prudent move. In fact, I truly believe gold and silver will turn out to be the investment winners for the decade of 2010-2020. To help offer that reassurance, I will quickly touch on some of the reasons gold and silver will grow in popularity over the years.

'Fiat' versus 'real'. Gold and silver are real money and have been for over 5000 years. Unfortunately, today the U.S. dollar and all currencies around the world are 'fiat' currencies, which means they are not backed by the intrinsic value and benefits that gold and silver offer. In fact, fiat currencies have no intrinsic value at all. Instead, these currencies are only paper and ink which all governments now print and order their citizens to use as money ('fiat' mean government decree). As you are probably aware, paper money is easily printed in ever larger quantities. And you are also probably aware that more printed money causes that currency to become devalued over time. This key point is vitally important and a basic money principle worth repeating, *the more fiat currency, the less good and services that currency buys.*

As investors the world over wake up to the fact that their money is buying less and less, they will move out of dollar type investments and into sound money and assets. Gold and silver will be at the top of their list. Make it yours too.

'Physical' versus 'paper'. I am far from an expert on the gold and silver paper market but feel it is important for you to know the difference between the two. To begin with, understand if you can buy and hold your precious metals, you are buying 'physical' precious metals. If you buy and can't actually hold your precious metals, you are buying 'paper', meaning some kind of traded precious metal fund. My understanding is the paper market has been extremely manipulated for years, generally forcing and keeping precious metal prices lower than they should be. It is also my understanding that this manipulation is being exposed for what it is. Experts say that when the exposure officially hits the fan, gold and silver prices could double, triple, or more; literally overnight. You want to own and hold your gold and silver .If you wish to learn more about precious metals manipulation, read the writings of Ted Butler, recognized as the leading expert on this subject. His website is: www.butlerresearch.com.

Industrial demand keeps rising. This applies much more to silver than gold. Constantly changing technology keeps leading to new usages for silver. In fact, you might be surprised to learn that the only natural resource with more uses than silver is oil! Oil has about 30,000 patented uses and silver follows with 10,000 uses. In addition, there are currently more patent applications for silver than all other base metals combined. You also may be surprised to learn that silver is employed in the following products or industries; bandages, batteries, water storage, washing machines, CDs, cell phones, computers, light switches, and anything else electronic. Then there are solar panels, skyscraper glass, mirrors, food processing, film, bearings, automobiles and clothing, the list goes on and on.

Unfortunately, all these usages lead to a two fold problem. First, most of these usages require such small quantities of silver that we can't or won't bother to recycle it. This means every time we toss out an old cell phone, computer, T.V., or even socks, we are tossing out much needed and unsalvageable silver, resulting in continually shrinking supplies.

At the same time supplies are shrinking, we have China, India, and most other countries striving to enjoy the same luxuries the average American has taken for granted for decades. Billions of people world wide now want what 330 million U.S. citizens have enjoyed. This new demand will put astronomical pressure on a silver market already buckling under the strain of current demand. I see nothing but much higher silver demand fighting with dwindling silver supplies in the future; so much so that one day, we may run out of the world's most useful metal.

Precious metals are rare. Even though both gold and silver fall in this category, they are different animals. Let's look at both of them.

GOLD. Gold is just rare, period. Because of this rarity, gold has earned the respect and privilege to be primarily used as coins and jewelry. Those two uses virtually guarantee gold's existence and preservation. Simply said, almost all the gold ever mined can still be accounted for unless it is sunken treasure somewhere at sea. The simple fact is, gold is rare and everyone the world over recognizes that fact. Gold will always have intrinsic value.

SILVER. Silver is different than gold. Yes it is rare, but nowadays, a lot of that rarity comes from the industrial uses previously mentioned. And, as previously mentioned, world wide, yearly silver usage is increasing to the point that the mining industry is unable to keep up.

This is not a new problem. Silver production lagging behind actual usage has been going on for decades. For example, in the 1950's, there was estimated to be about 5 billion ounces of investment grade silver above ground. Sixty years later, it is believed that we have less than 1 billion ounces left. That is a loss of 80% of investment grade silver! Because of this increased demand and lost supply, some experts predict we may run out of silver by 2030. Others say we won't run out of silver, but they predict silver will become more rare and valuable than gold! Which prediction is closer to the truth? Only time will tell.

Population is increasing. World population has crossed the 7 billion mark and is still growing fast. In fact, world population is estimated to hit 10 billion by the year 2050, with some experts saying 10 billion is a conservative number! Whatever the population grows to, all those people will need food, housing, clothing, and jobs. They will also want the luxuries of life. Every one of those needs and luxuries for every one of those people will require an abundance of natural resources to fulfill. Resources such as iron ore, oil, wheat, cotton, water, silver, and much, much more. This means that commodities and natural resources should do very well as investments in the future. The problem is most of these items can't actually be bought and held by the investor. This would require large storage spaces and preservation techniques most investors don't have. Imagine trying to store 55 gallon drums of oil, or cotton, or even wheat! Impossible! Gold and silver on the other hand, store easily and can be preserved forever.

Available Products

Now that you are armed with the reassurance of why gold and silver should prove to be a sound future investment for you and your loved ones, you must decide what form of gold and silver you are going to purchase. Let's quickly take a look at some of the actual products you can choose from.

Pure Bullion. Sure you can acquire gold and silver by purchasing jewelry, old candlesticks, or even inheriting your grandma's antique silverware, but in doing so, you're purchasing them the hard way. Nowadays, you can buy your precious metal bullion by the ounce (bullion, by the way, is the industrial term for refined, uncoined physical gold and silver).

Gold and silver are sold based on a 'troy' ounce, with a troy ounce equaling 31.1 grams. Every bullion dealer now carries gold and silver products in 1, 5, 10, 100, or even 1000 troy oz. bars. All these products are made out of pure gold or silver as recognized by '.999' displayed somewhere in the product.

In addition to bars, all dealers sell 'rounds'. These coin looking pieces are appropriately nicknamed as these products are flat and round, closely resembling old silver dollars. It should be noted however, that rounds are not legal tender and never will be. They are simply another choice when purchasing .999 gold or silver.

Unfortunately, many people have an interest in buying gold and silver bullion but lack the funds to purchase full ounces of these precious metals, especially gold. The mints that produce these fine products have finally woken up to this fact and their answer was to offer bars and rounds in smaller sizes produced in quarter, and half ounces. Some offer even smaller products based on gram weights.

One ounce legal tender coins. If legal tender coins are your interest, there are some countries that produce gold and silver coins in one ounce sizes. The most popular are:

- U.S. American Eagles
- Canadian Maple Leafs
- Vienna Philharmonics
- African Krugerrands

All these are recognized as legal tender, although you will not want to use them at face value as their gold and silver content far exceeds their denominational worth.

In the past, I tended to stay away from these coins as they carried a much higher per ounce price than rounds or bars. Higher per ounce prices went against my strategy of buying the most precious metals for my money. Besides, I was only purchasing gold and silver products for their metals content. Lately however, I have taken an increased interest in U.S. Eagles and 1 ounce legal tender coins because many states are working on legislation recognizing the true value of gold and silver coins as legal tender.

For instance, some states are talking of eliminating the capital gains tax on the sale of such coins. Others are recognizing the market value of these coins based on their precious metal content instead of their face value, thereby giving them monetary value based on their precious content. Because of this new legislative interest, it is quite possible that gold and silver will gain future monetary power no matter what happens in the economy. This is another area that only time will tell.

Old U.S. silver coins. You may also choose to buy old silver U.S. minted coins. The most popular and recognized of these coins were all manufactured before 1965 and include dimes, quarters, half and full dollars. Even though they are regular U.S. minted coins and you could use them anywhere top make a purchase, you seldom see them in circulation. Why? Because the value of the silver in those coins far exceeds their face value, so when someone who understands their true worth finds one, they quickly take it out of circulation..

The most popular of these coins, include dimes, quarters, half and full dollars all minted before 1965, are labeled as 90% silver coins because their metal content is 90% silver and 10% other base metals. The 10% base metals weren't added to save silver usage during production, but were added to give the coins long lasting durability for every day use. After the government stopped producing 90% coins, they produced a Kennedy half dollar that was 60% copper and 40% silver. These are appropriately referred to as '40%' coins and were minted between 1965 and 1969. Many people elect for the 90% coins over the 40% ones when purchasing old silver coins, but I believe, as silver becomes increasingly rare, interest in these coins will rise. You can buy these coins individually or in bags up to 1000 dollars in face value.

Prices and Premium

The gold and silver daily prices in the market are called 'spot' price. Generally the spot price will move up or down numerous times during the day. You, as an everyday buyer, will not get to buy at 'spot'. Instead, you will pay a price higher than the listed spot. This difference between your higher price and the spot price is called 'premium'. The reason for the premium is simple; you will most likely purchase your precious metals from some kind of business, and that business needs to make a profit. The premium covers that profit.

In today's current market, the mark-up over spot is right around 3-7%, with silver's mark-up a little higher than gold's.. This pricing is for .999 fine products only: it does not include American Eagle government minted coins. American Eagles are looked at differently. Since Eagles are the only official gold and silver coin currently minted by the U.S. government and therefore are officially money, dealers ask higher premiums for them.

90% and 40% silver coins are priced differently than .999 fine. For one reason, these coins don't have a full ounce of silver in them, so the per ounce price is seldom used. Instead, prices are a multiple of face value. Once you determine which you are purchasing, 90% or 40%, you will be given a multiple, which represents the coin's "melt" value. Then you simply take that figure and multiply it times the face value you wish to buy, and you have your purchase price. You can learn more about old coins and their melt values @ www.coinflation.com

Start with silver

In case you haven't noticed, I have given a little more attention to silver than gold. It's not that I don't like gold, because I do. It's just that I believe silver has more of an upside to it, therefore offering more 'bang for the buck'. You too might want to consider beginning your purchases with silver. Here are a few reasons why;

Silver is undervalued compared to gold. It has been estimated that in the earth's crust, the natural ratio of silver to gold is 16:1, In other words, sixteen ounces of silver in the ground for every ounce of gold. If that is true, you would think that you could buy either 16 ounces of silver or 1 ounce of gold at the same market price, right? Wrong. As I write these words, the silver to gold market price ratio is approximately fifty to one! This means you can buy either 50 ounces of silver or 1 ounce of gold for an equivalent price. What a bargain! 50 ounces for the price of 16! Now I'm not the fastest race car on the track, but even *I* realize that anytime I can purchase 50 ounces of silver for the same price as 16, then silver is on sale; and I have always liked a good sale!

The important thing to understand is this: chances are, as silver becomes more rare, that ratio will work its way back to, and possibly even surpass, the natural ratio of 16:1. In fact, it would not surprise me in the least if the ratio got closer to 10:1, especially considering the higher demand versus depleting supplies that lie ahead. But until that time arrives, I will continue to make silver my buying choice when it comes to precious metals.

Second, if you are like the average Joe (or Joann), it can be extremely difficult to come up with the current 1700-2000 dollars required to purchase an ounce of gold. Two thousand dollars is a lot of money, no matter how you slice it, and for many families, it is close to their total monthly household income.

On the other hand, with a little effort, most people can scrape together the 30-40 dollars per ounce it currently takes to purchase an ounce of silver, theoretically making 1 ounce of silver obtainable to the greater population, whereas 1 ounce of gold is not. So it stands to reason that as more and more people wake up to the true value of precious metals and decide to begin purchasing some of their own, silver will be their first logical choice. This factor alone will help drive prices continually higher.

It's really a savings account. The financial stability of the world has never been more compromised. Many experts believe that without immediate action, our dollar, and many other currencies around the world, will either partially or totally collapse in the next few years. A brief look at world monetary history can verify their thinking. Many of the strongest countries though out history have had their monetary policies fail at some point, only to be replaced with a new system. In most instances, that system had some kind of tie to gold and silver.

Personally, at worst, I believe a partial' if not total collapse is possible. At best, I believe we are headed to massive inflation caused by the enormous amounts of fiat money and debt that has been created over the last few years. I'm not just talking about the United States. I believe most countries will be prone to this problem. Therefore, I now view my precious metals as a hedge against inflation as well as a savings account. I keep enough cash available to pay 2-3 months of bills: everything else gets turned into sound assets, generally gold and silver.

This seems to have been a wise move. I started buying when silver was $12 per ounce, really stocked up when it fell to $8 per ounce, and today my average cost is about $16 per ounce, far below the current market value. This means my 'savings account' has earned exceptional interest in the 5 years I've held it. Plus as a bonus, I figure, if I run short of money I can always dip in my 'savings' to bail me out.

Silver is easier to divide. Another good reason to begin with silver that it's easier to divide than gold. Here's what I mean: let's say you can purchase either 1 ounce of gold or 50 ounces of silver. You choose silver. Five years later, the financial crisis is at its worst and you need to sell a little of your precious metals holding to pay some overdue bills. Since you bought silver over gold, you can sell 1 or 2 ounces and leave the rest of your holdings untouched, thereby helping to ensure that you don't spend more than planned. Plus there is something psychologically reassuring about not cashing in $2000 worth of gold to pay off a $50 or $100 debt.

Also, as previously mentioned, keep in mind that more people will be able to come up with the cash to buy an ounce of silver easier than they could gold. This automatically gives you a much larger market when you decide to sell.

In addition, with more ounces where each ounce is worth less, it is easier to hide your net worth in smaller portions. For example, let's say you have 1 ounce of gold as your nest egg. You hide it where you are certain no one will ever find it. But low and behold, one day while you are at work, a burglar breaks in and, using a metal detector, finds your gold coin. You've lost 100% of your holdings.

On the other hand, let's say you've purchased 50 silver rounds and have stashed them in 5 different spots around your house or property. There is a good chance that your metal detector wielding burglar will find only 1 or 2 portions of your hidden treasures then leave believing he's got it all. You will feel violated but also happy that you hid your stash in multiple locations. Yes, it is a terrible feeling to be robbed of a part of you portfolio, but it feels worse to lose it all!

Silver is the only asset priced lower than its' 1980s peak. If you look at today's prices of things, especially investments, and then compare those prices to 30 or so years ago, you will notice that most prices are much higher today. Oil is though the roof. Stock prices have risen tremendously. Housing prices, even though they have severely dropped the last few years, are still much higher than they were in 1980. Even gold has doubled and it is just warming up in its climb. But silver; as of this writing, is still roughly 30% *below* its all time high, and that's even with silver demand rising as supplies evaporate! It is probably this paragraph, more than any other, which should make you think heavily about purchasing silver over gold.

Part II

Ah, we're finally here. We are finally at the portion of the book that the title refers to. It is here where I hope to give you the necessary tips to formulate a precious metals buying plan that is feasible enough to work with your individual needs. Some of these tips offer insight on finding, earning, or freeing up the cash to make gold and silver purchases. Other tips are to help relieve anxiety build up as you learn to maneuver your way though some of the potential pitfalls. And a few tips are just bits of advice I believe you should know. Your objective is to sift through these tips and use any and all that will get you the precious metal portfolio you dream of and rightfully deserve.

Tips on funding your purchases

Have you ever bought a house or a car using financing? You put a small percentage down and the lender loans you the rest. Now go try to get that same kind of funding to purchase gold and silver. It's not going to happen. Not from a bank anyway. Therefore, if you want to purchase precious metals, it's almost guaranteed that you will be putting up 100 percent of the purchase price. Since funding the precious metals purchase is so important, I decided to begin this section with tips on finding the cash for those purchases, then following them up with tips on the actual buying process and pertinent information to increase your chances of success.

Alter your Budget. When hoping to make a purchase not typical of your lifestyle and needs, the budget is the first place one looks for the extra cash. However, your budget may be stretched to the max, or at least you think it is. But I bet every one of you could make changes in your current spending habits that would free up the money to buy one ounce of silver a week. If it can't be weekly, then I'm positive it could be done monthly.

If you're like most people, you go to work, earn your paycheck, and then come home and spend it without a clue of how much gets spent and where. Yeah, I realize you know some of it to the penny, but there is a large percent that just goes out for useless everyday expenses. Do you really know *where* that goes, how often, and how much? I'd bet you don't!

So try this for a month. Every time you buy something you don't *honestly* need, get a receipt. Buy a candy bar at 7-11, get a receipt. Stop for a newspaper and cappuccino in the morning, get a receipt. Pass the library to buy a book at the bookstore, get a receipt. Spend four times what you should have on a pair of boots, get a receipt. At the end of thirty days, look at your receipts. What do you see? Is there a pattern? Is there anything you could cut back on, or even do without? Less candy or cappuccino maybe? How about those boots? 4 times, *really*? I'll wager that if you look close enough, there is a very good chance you will discover that you *can* free up a few dollars here and there to put toward your gold and silver purchases.

Next, look over your bigger lifestyle: what can you change that you'd barely miss? Can you cut your cable package back to the basics? Can you eat out less? How about substituting hot dogs for steak or pork chops twice a week? Maybe put on long sleeves and turn the thermostat down? Go on a 3 day local vacation instead of that 7 day cruise?

Take time to understand and organize your spending habits and alter them wherever you can. Learn to barter with your neighbors. Car pool or take public transportation. Visit your local library for books and movies. Buy in bulk and stock up. Look for going out of business sales and take advantage. I recently hit such a sale and bought six pairs of steel toed work boots shoes for $100.

Usually, if you look hard enough, there's always something you can adjust, leaving a few dollars for your precious metal buying. I have come to the definite conclusion that if you truly believe the window for purchasing precious metal is small and the time to buy is now, and you *really* want in, you will find a way to trim your budget.

Get a second income. Many of you may argue that this doesn't qualify as a 'tip'. You could be correct, but I will say that this tip played an important role in developing my portfolio, and if possible, I strongly recommend you go this route, especially if you've gone over your budget with a fine tooth comb and really can't slice it any thinner. You see, I've had gold and silver on my radar for several years. In fact, I still try to read something on the precious metals every day. One of the things I've learned and truly believe is that you may see precious metals rise at astronomical rates of speed in the near future. Whether this happens next month, next year, or five years from now, nobody really knows for sure. But in the case of buying precious metals, I think it would be far better to be 5 years to early than a few days to late. If you believe in this possibility of prices taking off to the degree that I do, you may want to purchase as much gold and/or silver as fast as you can.

In *Part I*, you may recall, I mentioned why I believe gold and silver, especially silver, will be the strongest investment this decade. Now what if I said that it is possible, when silver reaches its bubble, and some day it *will* bubble, that at that peak, you might be able to buy a medium sized family home with only 300 to 500 ounces of silver? Sounds far fetched doesn't it? It might be, but those who understand the silver market think it is a definite possibility. Notice I said *possibility* not probability, it's possible. Personally, I don't know, but I think it's worth the gamble to try and own enough silver in case that prediction comes true.

To take this thought process a little further, let's say that you agree and have figured out a way to buy 5 ounces of silver per month, or 60 ounces a year, and you've set a goal of purchasing 300 ounces total. If the price doesn't increase at all, thus decreasing the number of ounces purchased each month, in five years, you will have your 300 ounces. It will take 8 years and 4 months to make the 500 ounce goal, and that's if prices stay low and you never miss or skip a month.

Now what happens if gold and silver explode 1 year after you start buying? How will you feel? How will it affect your buying? How about your goal? My guess is, you will possibly stop buying and stall out at 60 ounces. Sure that's probably much more silver than most people will have accumulated, but you're not most people. *You* set a goal remember? But unfortunately, 60 ounces is a far cry from the original goal you were shooting for.

However, what if you took on an evening job 2, maybe 3 nights a week, or worked Saturdays, and dedicated all those paychecks toward your goal? Almost any small part time job should help you purchase an additional 20 ounces a month provided you don't go and spend it on crap you think you deserve because you are now working harder. Anyway, 20 extra ounces a month brings your total purchase to 25 ounces every 30 days. At that rate, in one year, you will have amassed your original goal, 300 ounces. And, chances are, once you settle into that second job and reanalyze your situation, you will realize it wasn't that difficult to do and hardly put a strain on your life at all.

So, with all that said and done, the $100,000 question becomes, is it worth it to you to devote two evenings a week or so to increase your odds of reaching your goal before the precious metals explode?

I can't answer for you, but for me, that answer turned out to be a resounding YES!
I used this tactic in the beginning of my precious metals buying and it helped to build my portfolio *way* beyond my original goal. Plus, if you remember, I stated that my average price for an ounce of silver was only $16 dollars! Put another way, because I was willing to work harder than usual for a short period of time, and then applied those extra funds toward purchasing precious metals early in the upward price movement, I have tripled my original goal and I am in at a very low price. Truth be told, I still buy every month out of habit, but if prices exploded tomorrow, I could stop, secure in the knowledge I've exceeded my expectations.

Use your homes' equity to buy precious metals. Since 2008, the equity in many peoples' homes has dried up, so much so, that if they sold today, they might have to bring money to the closing table. However, there are some people who miraculously still have equity in their homes. If you are one of those folks, first, consider yourself fortunate, and second, seriously consider borrowing against that equity and purchasing some precious metals. Now I can almost hear you groan and I know what you're thinking. You are wondering why I'm suggesting you add another monthly payment to your already tight budget.

Before you get your feathers ruffled and walk away, hear me out. Currently, most home equity loans are in the neighborhood of 2-5 percent. This is at the same time real inflation is running around 6-7 percent, at the same time the government is claiming inflation is below 3 percent (I don't think anyone in the government actually buys their own food, clothes, or gasoline, otherwise they would know this 3% figure is laughable).

So if the government is claiming 3%, where did I get this inflation figure of 7-8 percent? I didn't make it up, that's for sure. Instead I pulled it from a website entitled 'shadowstats.com'. This excellent website is run by a man named John Williams. John knows that over the years, our government has changed their formulas for computing inflation, unemployment, and other government statistics. This didn't happen overnight. It took over 30 years to evolve into today's formulas.

John understands you can't compare one set of statistics with an altered set of statistics without having misleading information. He believes in comparing apples to apples, as do I, so he uses the unaltered formulas of old to calculate today's true figures before he does any comparisons. As I write these pages, he has computed today's inflation at 6%, which is higher than 3%, but down from the 9% he calculated in late 2008. Learn more about true government figures @ www.shadowstats.com.

Now let's get back to borrowing from your home' equity. If real inflation is 7% and you can borrow money to buy precious metal at 5%, it looks to me like you are actually making 2% purchasing power by borrowing against that equity! So apply this thinking to the precious metals. Last year gold was up around 14% (this figure varies depending on what twelve month time frame you use). Take away your 5% home equity costs and you're still ahead 9%. All because you took a few dollars and bought precious metals.

How is all this possible? Well, a few sentences back you learned the government is reporting artificially low inflation. They are performing this little scam at the same time they are keeping interest rates artificially low. These two combined government maneuvers are designed to make you believe our economy is slowly recovering. Since gold is inflation sensitive, the rising prices of gold tell you that a true recovery is an illusion.

So why not use this set of circumstances to your advantage? By borrowing dollars at a low interest rate and using them to purchase a strong asset like precious metals, you have an excellent chance of coming out smelling like a rose.

Another advantage is that you're not breaking your back every month trying to come up with the funds to purchase your precious metals, nor are you worrying every month that the gold and silver prices are going to go ballistic (someday soon, they will) leaving you short of your targeted goal.

With all that said, there are some precautions to consider;

- Don't borrow so much money that you can't make the scheduled payments.
- Since silver has a much lower price point and is grossly undervalued compared to gold, I would recommend purchasing *only* silver with this technique.
- Don't borrow to buy paper precious metals, buy only the physical.
- Don't use a high cost financing, like a credit card for this tip. Stay in the 3-6% range.

Cash in a CD in and buy precious metals. Right now in America, your Federal Reserve chairman is *telling* you they are planning to cause inflation over the next few years. He wants 2% and will do this by printing more fiat money thus causing the dollar to lose value. My question is' what if he misses? What if he takes us to an inflation rate of 6% instead of 2, especially as calculated by his formula versus the older one? Does that mean the consumer will be seeing true inflation rates of 15 percent in their groceries or at the pump? In their everyday living costs? And what about investments? If the Federal Reserve chairman is *telling* you they are planning to cause inflation over the next few years why, *why* in the world would you want to hold anything tied to paper money, like CDs or bonds?

Take my dear mother for example. For the last few years I have been trying to get her to trade in some of her CDs, which are currently earning around 1% interest. I would like her to place that money into gold or silver. 10 percent of her CDs are all I'm asking. To make it easy on her, I have even offered to do all the leg work. I would buy her precious metals, take delivery, and help her set up storage. I approach her about this every three months or so, but somehow; she always has a reason to refuse to do so, even as she has watched my precious metals double in the last four years! She says she's comfortable in CDs because they make her feel safe!

Parents! When will they ever learn to listen?

Ok, she won't listen to me but maybe you will. Why earn 1-2% on a measly piece of paper when you can increase your wealth 5-10 times faster with a tangible asset you can actually hold? You don't need to trade all your paper investment in, but I *strongly* encourage you to convert some of your CD wealth into precious metals.

Borrow from a friend or relative. Borrowing from family or friends is very seldom a good idea. In fact, I debated long and hard about mentioning it here. I eventually decided to go for it when I rationalized that you would be borrowing to purchase a very solid asset, versus borrowing to start a risky business, buy a car, or take a cruise. From the perspective of buying an asset, it made perfect sense. However, I want to add a word of caution; if you use this tip, don't get greedy. Be fair to your lender and only borrow what you can honestly pay back and *only* borrow if your 100% sure you won't hurt your relationship. Oh, and remember to give the lender your metals or some other asset as collateral for your debt.

Develop a precious metals fund. 5 years ago, when I first realized I needed to be purchasing precious metals, I would buy whenever I was able to set money aside (I had yet to make regular purchases a habit). Since then I have set aside an envelope that I put money in for the sole purpose of buying my silver. I fund that envelope in a variety of ways. Percentages of extra earned income, bonuses, money from a garage sale, eBay sales, even portions of birthday or financial windfalls have found their way into this envelope. A few dollars here and a few dollars there do add up. Now, if for some reason I can't make my regular precious metal purchase, I can fund it from this envelope. However, I have to level with you; because of using the tips in this booklet, I seldom need to use these funds for a bail out. Instead, I use the built up money to buy extra metals when their price dips. The secret to making this work is to *only* use this envelope money to purchase your gold or silver.

Tips with sound advice

I hope the previous tips have opened your eyes and thought process to come up with some creative ways to fund your precious metals purchases. Even though none are magical in their design, with practical application and effort, they do offer the desired results. Before we get into the actual buying process, review the following tips. They provide a little extra sound advice that will help make the buying journey easier.

Realize gold and silver are very volatile. Compared to other assets investors can park their money in, dollar for dollar, gold and silver, especially silver; are a really small percentage of the market. It does not take very much buying or selling to cause 10-20% price spikes and dips. It happens. In fact, it happens frequently. Get used to it. Don't let these dips shake you out of the market. Just remember, you are accumulating gold and silver for the long run and future bubble, so don't be too upset when you buy on Tuesday and on Wednesday the price drops 10%. Gold and silver prices are extremely volatile. Simply remind yourself of all the reasons you believe they are going higher in the future and keep the faith.

Avoid advice from well meaning but ill informed friends. For many years, gold and silver were so unloved, so unnoticed, so under the radar, that they laid dormant in most peoples minds. However, economical and political conditions are becoming turbulent and gathering strength, evolving into the perfect storm out on the future horizon.

Sadly, the general public is totally unaware of these conditions and the approaching storm, so they still base their gold and silver perception on an outdated calm and balmy past. If you wish to gather sound precious metals advice, study the guys who have lived and breathed this stuff for decades: Ted Butler, David Morgan, Mike Maloney, Eric Sprott. You will learn more from them in a week than your well meaning friends can tell you in a lifetime.

Don't ask a financial expert if you should buy gold or silver. It's not that I'm against financial planners because I'm not. It's just most of them turn into glorified salespersons after graduating from 'Stocks and Bonds' college. They learn phrases such as "overall, the stock market goes up". Or "at your age you should have x % of stocks and x % of bonds in your portfolio". These are all canned terms or advice. You see, most financial planners make their money off commissions and that means sales. They are trained to make sales, thus commissions, through the packaging of their companies products. Physical gold offers them no commission (gold stocks, yes; physical, no) so why suggest it?

My biggest issue however, is that most planners just advise their client using standard surface criteria without looking at the big and deeper picture and all the surrounding factors. A good financial planner looks at the past as well as the future in a variety of ways: political changes, legislative changes, business changes, demographic changes technology advances, current trends and the total economic picture. A good financial planner looks at current and future supply and demand needs and wants and which way those trends are headed. Then a good financial planner will analyze all this collected data before doling out investment advice.

To me, a good financial planner charges by the hour for their services and they make more money from their investments than they do from their job. A *really* good financial planner also understands fiat money and gold and silver's place in the economical world and its future.

Develop the habit. Life is full of habits. In fact, developing healthy habits help you take care of mundane but necessary day-to-day items. For example; flossing and brushing your teeth, taking out the garbage, changing your furnace filter, or emptying the litter box are all developed habits which make life a little easier, healthier, or pleasant.

Even though I alluded to it in previous pages, this one is worth mentioning again. Precious metals purchasing also need to be a habit. Make those purchases a regular weekly or monthly practice. Decide how much you're going to buy and how often. Write it as a goal and display it where you see it often throughout your day. Also make your purchase goal one your can easily achieve. Don't shoot for the moon here. Remember, in this case, less is better. These regulated purchases are too important to drop the ball on. It is far better to buy an ounce of silver once a week than to purchase ten ounces if and when you get the money.

Pay yourself first. Simply said, you need to buy some precious metal whether you think you can afford it or not. If you read any type of investment book, you have probably stumbled across this phrase. The *idea* behind the phrase is to religiously build up your savings and investment accounts for the future. The *philosophy* behind it is, if you pay yourself first, even if this payment leaves you short on your other bills, you will work harder to find the money to catch those late bills up. This then reinforces the habit of regularly putting away for your future. This is a tough habit to develop but the idea does work. The trick is, first, not to pay yourself such an outrageous amount that you will never be able to pay your regular costs of living; and second, to take action immediately to solve your money shortage issues when they creep up. Hustling up extra side work was one of the key ingredients in building my precious metals nest egg, and for doing it as quickly as I did.

Aim to own 10-20 percent of your net worth in precious metals. I don't know why, but buying physical gold and silver, is invigorating. It is addicting. The feel, the shine, and the ringing metallic sound they make when pinged; it all sucks you in. It starts to consume you. Soon you are looking for ways to acquire more and more. Theoretically, this is not necessarily a bad thing; however, you need to know when to let off the gas and coast on your buying of precious metals.

I suggest you think of slowing down your purchases when you reach your designated ounces or a certain dollar value. Experts say 10-20 percent of a person's net worth should be in the shiny stuff. Currently, this is probably a very reasonable goal, though keep in mind, as your net worth increases, so should your precious metals holdings. Also realize a sudden crisis, such as war or a severe economical collapse may be a reason to up those percentages. For now, aim for 10-20%.

Once you own it, keep it. Even though I know this is somewhat unrealistic, my personal goal is to pass my precious metals stash to my children upon my death. This means I plan to hold my precious metals for many years to come. As I have previously mentioned, with what I see on the financial horizon for our country and most countries around the world at this time, it makes the most sense to buy and hold. And I mean *hold with two hands*. I'm very concerned it could take a decade or two for true economic stability to reign once again I'm afraid to let go. And since I have studied the history of money, I know the importance gold and silver play during the recovery of major economic problems; they always come out on top! (*Beware:* Most economic "experts" have not studied money throughout history and will often argue this fact)

Tips on purchasing

Start small. If your finances were anything like mine when I started purchasing, this might be your only option. This doesn't mean you can't buy, it just means buying is going to take some planning, extra work, budget rearranging, or an exercise in creative thinking. No matter how weak your funds might be, buying is not impossible. So please don't use the problem of low funds as an excuse to stay out of the game. Almost anyone can come up with the money for 1 ounce of silver if they really try. Plus, keep in mind; even though it may not seem like much, one ounce is better than no ounces. And for some reason, once you obtain that first ounce, the second ounce becomes easier as does the third. Remember, Chicago wasn't built in a day (Rome is so cliche).

If you happen to be one of the lucky dogs that can start by purchasing hundreds of ounces at once, I applaud you, but I also want to warn you to please take heed. Go slow the first time out. It's not a horse race! Take a little time to learn the precious metals game and the rules that apply before you buy large quantities. Give yourself a little time to build your gold and silver knowledge, and consequently, confidence in yourself. It won't take long.

This is really two fold advice. Obviously you want to understand your subject matter so you aren't taken for a ride. The old rule "buyer beware" really applies here, and the best way I know for the buyer to beware is to learn the subject matter. Knowledge is a powerful thing.

The not so obvious part of the "take it slow" advice is this; if you have the funds to purchase 100-500 ounces of, let's say silver, you will probably be purchasing that order from one of the bigger national dealers. You will either do this by phone or over the internet. Now, in case you don't know it, the industry's general rule is, you prepay for your order: all of it, 100 percent, up front, and when your funds clear, the dealer will begin processing your precious metals order. In other words, you are committing your personal trust and your personal funds 100% before the dealer takes a bit of action. Ouch! Talk about trust issues! However, I have discovered that this isn't the hardest pill to swallow. What gets you is the *wait* for your precious metals to actually arrive.

You see, currently you are in luck, because, there are dealers filling orders in 3-7 days. Back in 2008, wait time was often 8-10 weeks! And sometimes the estimated delivery time came and buyers were receiving calls saying their order would be a few more weeks before arrival. I know I did. Now the first 1 or 2 times you've dropped hundreds, or most likely thousands of dollars on a prepaid order, every night, lying in bed can be hell, because you wake up thinking about your gold and silver order. You keep wondering if you made a huge mistake, and if you will ever receive your gold or silver. Rest assured, eventually the order arrives, fulfilled correctly, and sleep will once again become a part of your life.

Buy bigger orders after you've learned the ropes and are confident in the gold and silver market and its dealers.

Purchase old silver coins. In today's weakened economy, coming up with enough extra cash to purchase an ounce of silver may be difficult. If you fall into this category, there is another alternative: you can buy old silver coins. This allows you to purchase silver in even smaller increments than 1 ounce and at cheaper prices

Unlike investment grade silver, pre-1964 silver U.S. coins, such as dimes, quarters, half and full dollars, were all made for everyday use and minted using 90 percent silver and 10% other metals. Because these coins are not .999 percent pure, they are labeled "dirty" silver. Let me reassure you, there is nothing dirty about them. Old silver coins have 10 percent less silver content, but they are still a very valuable asset to have. For starters, these coins are familiar and easily recognized. They are also easy to purchase. And they will rise in value as silver rises in value.

Use 'dollar cost averaging' to purchase your metals. Dollar cost averaging works like this; if you have 100 dollars to buy silver with every month and this month silver costs $33 an ounce, you buy 3 ounces. Next month, the silver price dips to $25 per ounce so you get to purchase 4 ounces instead of 3. The third month, silver prices spike to $40. Now you can't even buy 3 ounces.... So what? Take your $100 and buy what you can. Remember, your *first* and main goal is to accumulate gold and silver on a regular basis. I repeat, *on a regular basis.* By using the dollar cost averaging technique to do so, you accumulate your precious metal holdings month after month, consistently adding to your pile. Don't try to time the market. It does work for some people, but I advise you not to try to it until you have built up your personal supply and feel educated on the precious metals market.

Buy on the dips. Here I am, one paragraph later, contradicting what I said in the previous paragraph. Well, yes I am and no, I'm not. You see, in the beginning, you need to develop the weekly or monthly habit of purchasing your metals, period. I'm not changing my stance on that previous tip because this regular buying habit is extremely important. I only suggest this particular tip for when you figure out a way to bring in extra funds for purchasing your gold and silver. Then, and only then, should you use any extra funds you might have to buy when the prices fall.

The main reason I don't want you to only buy on dips is that when will you buy your precious metals if the dips stop, or the dip isn't low enough for you? Believe me, the time is coming when the masses will wake up and head to gold and silver in droves. And like any investment driven by the masses, they will push precious metals into a bubble, probably a huge bubble. The problem is; no one knows how soon that time will arrive or how big it will actually get. It could begin next month, next year, or five years from now, and when it ends, who knows where the peak price will end up. When this day *does* arrive, you my friend, do not want to stand there watching, short of your precious metals goal, wishing you had purchased regularly instead of timing dips. Personally, I buy my minimum every month, and buy extra on the dips when I have the funds.

Play the game 'dry' first. Before you take that big leap and plunk down your hard earned cash practice the part of the buyer. Sit down and call several jewelry stores, coin shops, and pawn dealers in your area and ask some basic questions. Do the same with some of the dealers on the internet. Write down their answers so you can compare dealers later. A few starter questions might include;

- What's today's spot price?
- What's your premium over spot?

- Do you have any gold or silver American Eagles?
- What is your premium for these?
- Do you have 90% or 40% silver coins?
- What's the cost per face value?
- Any quantity discounts today?

As you practice your phone interview skills, take notes. I promise, if you do this 2-3 times a week for a couple of weeks, you will be much better prepared and more confident when you actually go to purchase your precious metals.

Tips on Dealers and Products

Buy known branded products. Believe it or not, there are frauds, scams, and counterfeit products in the precious metals market (yeah, I know, hard to believe). In the beginning, buy name brand products like American Eagles, Canadian Maple Leafs, Pan American, or Engelhard. Some of the larger dealers, such as Northwest Territorial Mint, also mint their own high quality products in addition to the other recognized names they sell. You will also see an Indian head/ buffalo tail round that is very popular among dealers because, even though it is .999 fine, it sells extremely well.

In the beginning, I recommend staying away from trinkets and specialty commemorative pieces unless stamped .999 and you know the exact weight, and therefore the real price, you are paying per ounce. Know what you are buying.

Use reputable dealers. Unless you buy from a close friend or relative or purchase your gold and silver off eBay (I wouldn't recommend doing either until you've learned the ropes), you will probably purchase your precious metals from a dealer.

If you purchase online, (which really is as easy as buying a book from Amazon) make sure the dealer has a high Better Business Bureau (BBB) rating. One of the fastest ways I've discovered to do this is using a website called www.goldshark.com. This great site lists dealers in order starting with the least expensive pricing first. Also listed will be the dealers BBB rating, estimated shipping time, if they take credit cards, and their dollar limits, if any apply.

Know what you want. Before you buy online or from a local dealer, know what you want to purchase and then try and stay the course. It could be a first choice with 1 or 2 alternatives such as; "I'm going to purchase 5 silver American Eagles, or 5 ounces of silver bullion, and if nothing else, 100 dollars of 90% silver coins." Knowing what you want provides confidence and keeps you focused because I guarantee you, the first couple of times you buy you will have forgotten most of what you learned from this book.

Know your spot price. Personally, I check spot prices two times a day, even during the weeks I have no intention of buying. This keeps me focused and aware of the market. That way, if gold and silver take a major dip or spike, I know it and can respond if I so choose. Plus, should I spontaneously walk into a dealer and decide to buy, I'm not using yesterday's prices to evaluate and negotiate my purchase.

Watch your premiums. I've noticed lately a big increase in ads selling specialty gold or silver coins, or even American Eagles, at *outrageously* inflated prices. Often these coins are in honor of a specific event, person, or place, and are advertised as a limited edition minting. What the ad is doing is playing two angles of good investment criteria. The ad hopes to entice buyers with the fact their product is gold or silver *and* also collectable, hence worth the obnoxiously inflated premium.

Coincidently, while polishing this section of the book, I took a break to flip though a national magazine. About 15 pages in was an ad for a 1 ounce silver 'collector' piece. It's price? Three times over spot! Of course the collector piece came with a display case (a fancy box) and a paper of authenticity probably making the 3 times spot a real bargain! Hmmmm. Maybe I *should* buy.

Hopefully you can tell I'm being facetious. Forget the collector element, that's not your interest. You are buying gold and silver for one reason and one reason only, their precious metal content. The collectability of that special coin will not matter at all when you decide to sell. I know this for a fact as I have many of these so called 'collectables' in my precious metals stash. *All* were purchased over the counter from a jewelry or coin dealer at the going market rate for its precious metal content. *None* were ever sold to me at collector prices *nor* did the dealers ever try to sell them to me at those prices. The dealers always showed them to me as precious metals prices; spot plus premium. If you wish to deal with collectable and special coins, get into coin collecting.

So when you find yourself holding a specially minted commemorative piece and your heart starts racing because you are looking and holding a 'collector' item, remember the basics. What kind of precious metals are you buying? How many ounces? What's the spot price per ounce? What percentage over spot are you paying? Is it in line with today's market? Don't buy into collector pieces, they just aren't worth it.

This caution is not just geared to gold and silver ads. I have experienced different jewelry/coin dealers with drastically different mark-ups, especially when the metals market was heating up after the 2008 financial crisis.

One last thought on dealers, should you purchase from a jewelry store, coin dealer, or other brick and mortar store, know their reputation. Have they been around awhile or are they new to the area? Do you think they will be in business tomorrow? Any complaints listed with the local Better Business Bureau? Ask around. Find out who gives good customer service and who doesn't.

Know all purchasing costs. The big moment has finally arrived. You're going to make your first purchase. You're on the phone with one of the dealers. You've decided to buy 10 one ounce silver rounds at $35 each. Your palms are sweaty! It's going to be difficult, but you're ready to cut loose with $350 of your hard earned cash. Suddenly, the salesperson quotes you a price higher than 350 dollars! Your heart drops. Why the increase in price?

Depending on how you buy and from whom, there could be hidden fees showing up in the final purchase price. They could be commissions, delivery charges, wire transfer fees, or credit card fees. Asking about commissions and delivery fees are some great questions for your dry runs, especially if you're interviewing internet dealers. All could be legit costs, but any extra fees mean you are paying a higher per ounce price. You need to be aware of all costs before the payment is agreed upon or sent.

Storing your precious metals

Once you've taken possession of your gold and silver, you will be faced with the need to store it. There are professional storage facilities that charge a premium and lock your precious metals in industrial sized vaults with top security. However, these can be expensive for someone just starting out in building up a precious metal portfolio. It would be of more financial benefit to you to look into this kind of security when your portfolio becomes worth100,000 dollars or more. Until then, it's up to you to keep your precious metal holdings safe. Take the following tips seriously.

Loose lips sink ships. Yes, I realize this is a war time saying, but it is sound, prudent advice worth mentioning. Keep your buying as secret as possible. Buy, hide, and shut up. Remember, the more who know you have it, the more who will find out you have it. Now, with that said, all rules have exceptions, including this one. I will explain with a couple of short stories. Over the last year or so, I have read 2 stories about construction workers unearthing stashes of gold and silver. The first involved workers demolishing an old shed. As they tore the ceiling down, a hoard of old silver coins fell from the sky. The second story happened in Russia. The scenario was almost identical except the shed was a mansion and the silver was gold. The really interesting thing about both these stories was, each stash was said to have a present market value of over 1 million U.S. dollars. I'm not suggesting that you tear out all your ceiling and walls looking for hidden treasure, but there is a moral here: *Don't hide your precious metal then die without telling anyone.*

You need to make sure someone you know and trust knows about your precious metals holdings should your plane go down tomorrow. For me, it's my wife: and because I'm aware that my wife and I could perish together, I also gave my brother a sealed envelope with a list of precious metals amounts and hiding places, just in case. I then added a copy to my safe deposit box should I get old and can't recall my hiding places, much like last year's Easter egg I can't seem to find.

Safe deposit boxes. For most people, their first storage choice will be a safe deposit box at their local bank. This is a good starting point but there can be drawbacks. First, you never know when the government will shut down the banking system for a period of time. They call this a 'bank holiday' (although it's no fun and is a pain in the rear. Oh, wait, that's just like a holiday). Anyway, remember 9/11? Banking, Wall Street, and most businesses closed for a few days. If we have an even larger major economical meltdown or an equivalent catastrophe, you may find you can't get to your metals when you want or need them the most.

Hiding at home. Because of the very slim, but very real chance of a catastrophe, I recommend keeping a percentage of your portfolio at home where you can grab it in seconds. What if there's a flood like hurricane Katrina or the tornadoes in Joplin, Missouri? If you had some of your metals at home, you could evacuate some of your wealth with you. There is a strong psychological benefit to knowing you have the ability to instantly provide financially for your family in a crisis.

Hiding at home, or your place of business if you are self employed, can be tricky. You must hide your gold and silver so it is well hidden from accidental detection by nosy friends and inquisitive children, as well as the professional thief. Finding those great hiding locations will tax your imagination. Start by taking a slow stroll though your house, garage, and around your property. Analyze everything. What has excellent nooks or crannies that most people would never dream are there? Make a list of potential hiding spots.

Let's start in the house, are there any household items that could double as undetectable storage, like an old piano, vacuum cleaner or antique sewing machine? Can you bury a few ounces of precious metals in 10 pounds of flour, sugar, or cans of coffee, placed high out of reach on the very top shelf of your pantry? Maybe you can wrap some in tin foil and label it 'whitefish', then shove it in your freezer.

Or how about the garage or shed? Can you hide your metals in the garage, maybe in a 50 pound box of nails or in that old motorcycle tank that's been on your top self for years? Do you have a shed that is a hotbed of hiding places? If you open your eyes and mind, you will find the hiding choices are endless.

Maybe you've combed the premises and you don't feel you have any good hiding spots, then go buy one. Go purchase an old vacuum cleaner, old gas tank, or sewing or computer monitor or tower. The trick is to make your hiding spots such a part of the natural surroundings that it would be silly for a thief to look there. There are additional security benefits if the item used for hiding is extra heavy, bulky and awkward to move, or really out of reach. You also might want to hide your precious metals in something partially made of steel to throw off metal detectors. A combination of these hints work best.

For example; replace the motor of an old dryer with your metals. Push the dryer in a hard to get to corner of the basement and throw a couple of heavy storage bins on top for good measure. Just don't make the hiding place something a thief would steal to resell, like a kid video game or cordless drill case. The main idea is to hide your silver (gold too) where even the sharpest minds would never suspect it.

It is important to also understand that most thieves who break into a house want to get in and out as fast as they possibly can. Often times, they will leave if they believe they found the majority of your stash. So I have adopted the philosophy of making it easy for them to find some stash! In other words, set them up! Help them accomplish their mission.

Because home invaders generally start their search in the master bedroom or home office, I chose to set my trap there. I have about 11 ounces of silver in a small *unlocked* safe (unlocked at all times) in my bedroom that only the winner of the 'Idiot-of-the-Year' award would miss! There are a few .999 rounds and a couple of 24 karat gold plated trinkets I bought for the sole purpose of becoming bait. Along with the silver are a few pieces of custom jewelry, a small box of wheat pennies, and $100 in cash. I've also added some official looking papers in envelopes that give the illusion of value. For instance, I've included instructions and phone numbers explaining where and how to cancel my credit cards if stolen. I supplement this information with *fake* visa numbers, *fake* expiration dates, and *fake* 3 digit codes found on the back of the cards. This gives the criminals something else of value to take, but costs me nothing!

Why do I set this bait? I believe once a robber has made the effort to enter my house, they probably won't leave until they find something of value or completely destroy my house trying. Why not make it easy on them? This way, they quickly find some goodies, and then hopefully leave before doing further damage. Plus, this technique offers an added safety benefit. If a robber breaks in when my family is at home, I or my wife can lead them to our treasures with out the added pressure of trying to remember hiding spots or a safe combination with a loaded weapon pointed at our heads.

When to stop buying

It is the nature of all investments to eventually reach a peak. I'm fairly sure this will apply to gold and silver one day, though I have no idea when that might be. Nobody likes to buy at the peak, unfortunately though, someone has to. The goal is to not let it be you! Therefore, you will want to develop some signs to watch for that might indicate a peak is drawing near. I have been studying precious metals and their surrounding circumstances for over 7 years now, and even though that doesn't make me an expert, it does give me confidence and insight on what I believe may be signs the peak is near. Here's my list:

- The U.S. and world governments actually balance their budgets, logically reduces debt and spending, and get debt to GDP ratios in line.

- The silver to gold ratio dips below 10 to 1. (Keep in mind this ratio may not apply if demand continues to outstrip supply and depletes silver to near extinction)

- It takes only 1-2 ounces of gold to purchase 1 share of the Dow. (In 2000, it took 43 ounces of gold to buy 1 share of the Dow. By 2010, it was 8 ounces. If gold explodes and/or the stock market crashes, it could take 2 ounces or less.)

- All my friends, neighbors, relatives, barber, paperboy, taxi drivers, grocery stockers, street vendors, and girl scouts tell me what "a wonderful investment they are making in gold and silver. It's a sure thing."

In other words, I'm not selling because I can make 10% in six months, or because that little sports car I've been ogling went up for sale. I'm waiting for the bubble, the big bubble that all investments eventually get. I am well aware that it could be years before the precious metal bubble actually arrives. I'm also very much aware that even though daily prices may go up and down like a well played yo-yo, overall, gold and silver prices have gone up for over a decade. Because of our debt and continual money printing, this is a trend that may continue for years to come. I plan to sell only when there is once again true financial stability in my country, a much better investment to sink my money in, or the personal need for survival forces me to sell. And then it will be using due diligence with extreme caution.

Understand, neither you nor I can predict the future. We can only make calculated and educated guesses. Anything could happen at any given moment. This anything could totally change your mind on how you view your precious metal holdings. For example, if tomorrow you hear on the news that someone has discovered how to turn iron ore into gold, you might want to sell that day. Or if gold and/or silver become the backing for currency once again, you may never wish to sell.

My point is that you need to educate yourself on the precious metals and its place in both the financial and industrial worlds. Then pay attention to what's going on in the world around you and analyze how that will affect your future and the future of precious metals. Don't stick your head in the sand, not when it comes to gold and silver.

The challenge

At the end of my introduction, I mentioned that I 'took the challenge and now felt like a king'. Well, I need to let you in on a little secret no one challenged me. I challenged myself. That challenge was to eventually purchase and hold 500 ounces of physical silver. Since that day when I threw down the gauntlet, I have amassed far past that amount. And I can honestly say, because I met my goal, I feel more financially secure than ever before and am back to sleeping at night.

I now challenge you to buy some precious metals. But because everyone faces different financial struggles and situations, I am not going to throw out specific ounces or dollar amounts for you to strive to purchase. Instead, I'm going to ask you to invest by percentages. I challenge you to find a way to take 2% of your monthly actual after tax income and buy precious metals with it each and every month for 6 straight months. You can adjust your income, get a second job, or use other ideas within these pages. The decision is yours.

Once that goal is complete, I challenge you to then up your goal to 5% of your monthly actual after tax income, and to use this percentage for the next 6 months. If you complete both of these goals, you will have devoted 12 months to buying gold and/or silver and should have your habits well established. You can then write your own challenges as you see fit.

I also want to add one more challenge. I challenge you to devote 2-3 hours a week to learning more about gold and silver, their role as money throughout history, and what is going on with the world's financial system. I challenge you to complete both these challenges for 1 year, and if you do, I promise, you will be well rewarded for doing so.

Thank you for reading this book. Good luck in your challenge.

Watch for my latest ebook;

"50 Hiding Places for Your Gold and Silver
(and other valuables)"

www.ingramcontent.com/pod-product-compliance
Lightning Source LLC
Chambersburg PA
CBHW071627170526
45166CB00003B/1228